Into the West

easy harp version

harp arrangement by Sylvia Woods   words and music by Howard Shore, Fran Walsh, and Annie Lennox

Moderately ♩ = 92

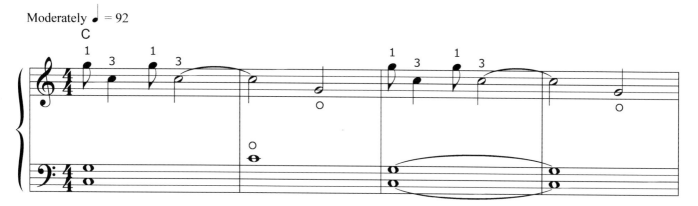

Verse 1

Lay down ... your sweet and wea-ry head

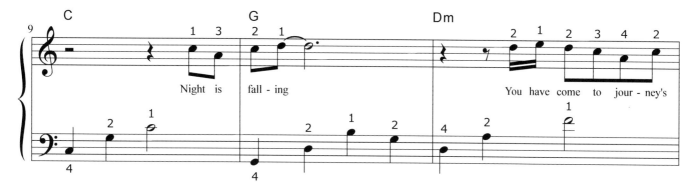

Night is fall-ing ... You have come to jour-ney's

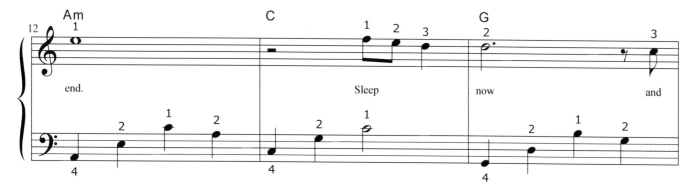

end. ... Sleep now ... and

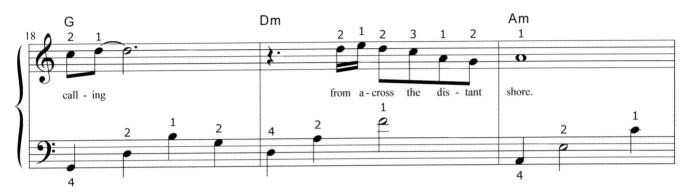

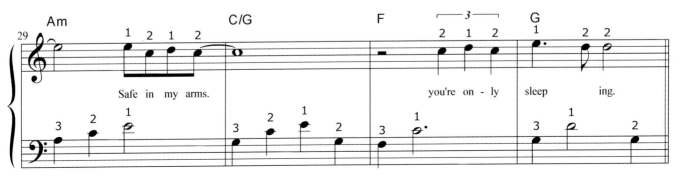

Chorus

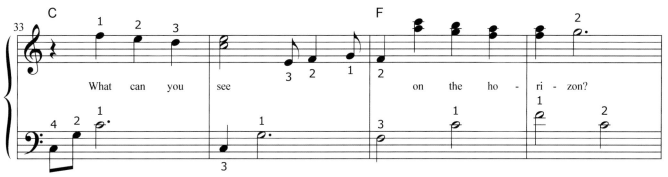

What can you see on the ho - ri - zon?

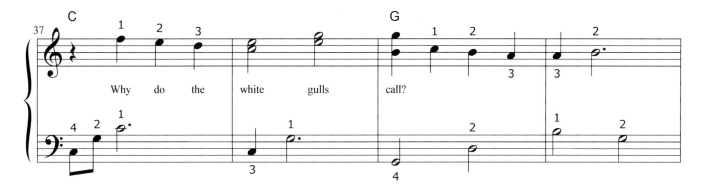

Why do the white gulls call?

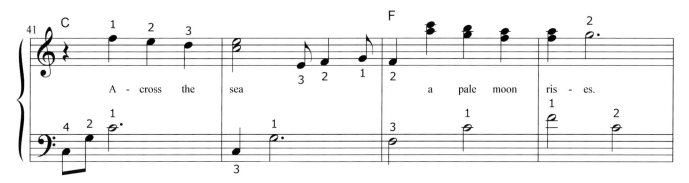

A - cross the sea a pale moon ris - es.

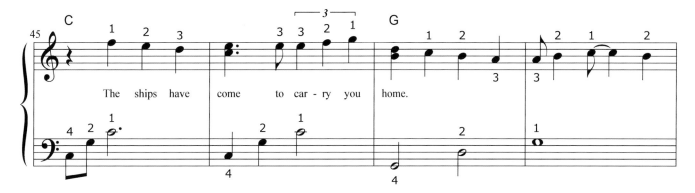

The ships have come to car - ry you home.

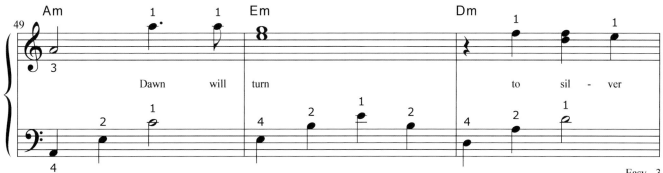

Dawn will turn to sil - ver

Easy - 3

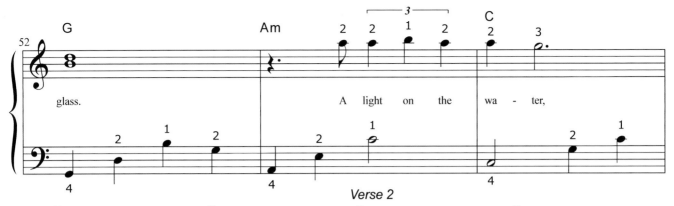

glass.　A light on the wa - ter,

Verse 2

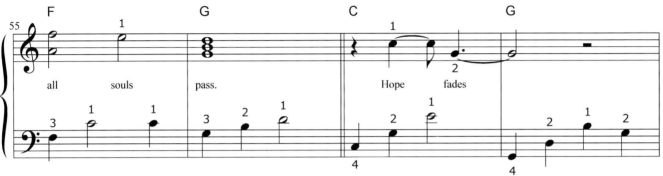

all souls pass.　Hope fades

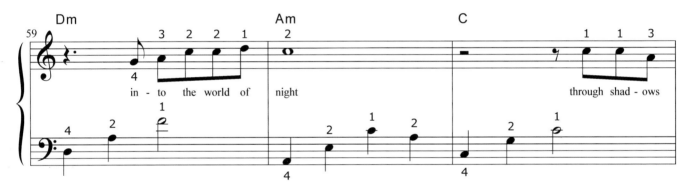

in - to the world of night　through shad - ows

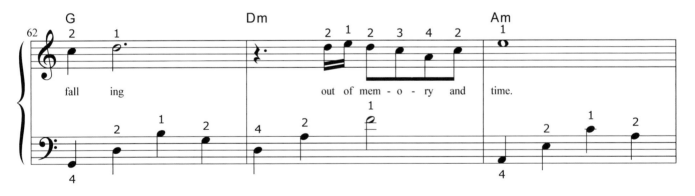

fall ing　out of mem - o - ry and time.

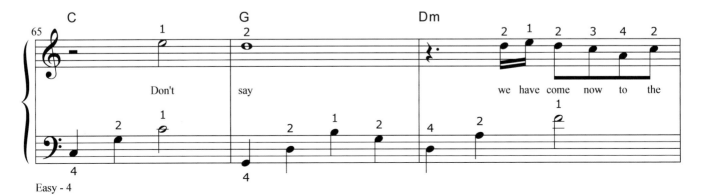

Don't say　we have come now to the

Easy - 4

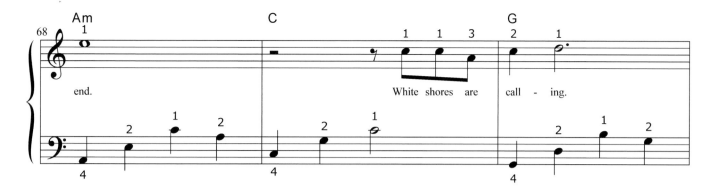

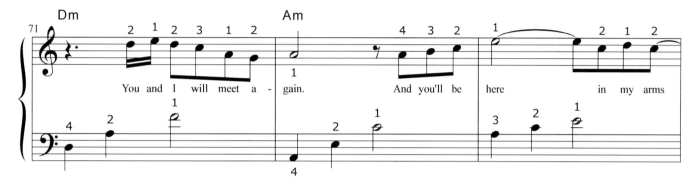

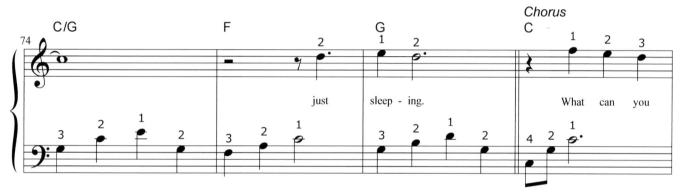

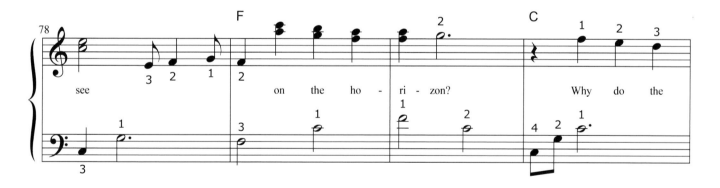

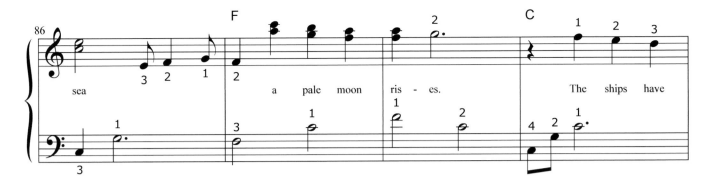

sea   a pale moon ris - es.   The ships have

come   to car - ry you   home.   And   all   will

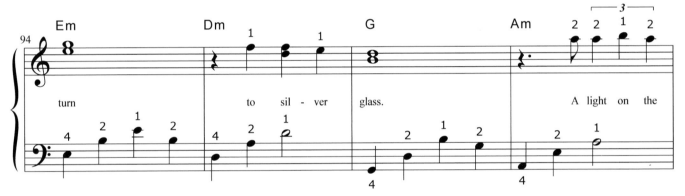

turn   to sil - ver glass.   A light on the

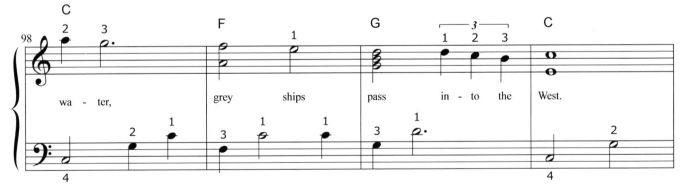

wa - ter,   grey ships   pass   in - to the   West.

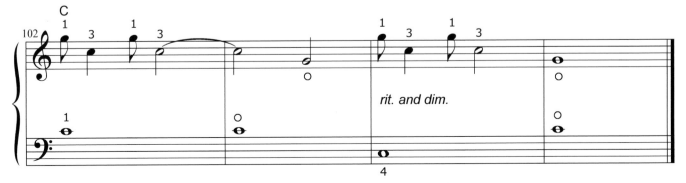

rit. and dim.

Easy - 6

INTO THE WEST
intermediate harp version

harp arrangement by Sylvia Woods — words and music by Howard Shore, Fran Walsh, and Annie Lennox

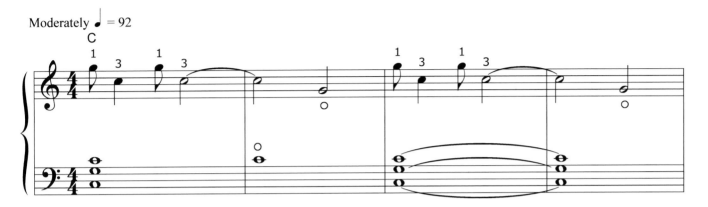

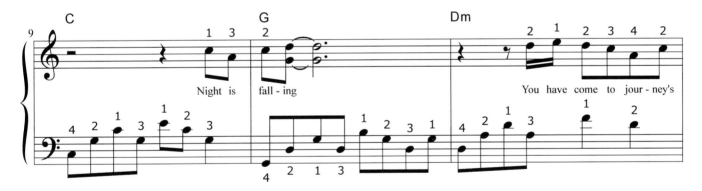

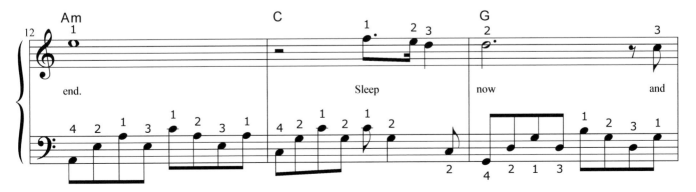

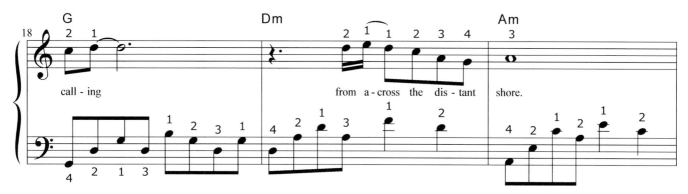

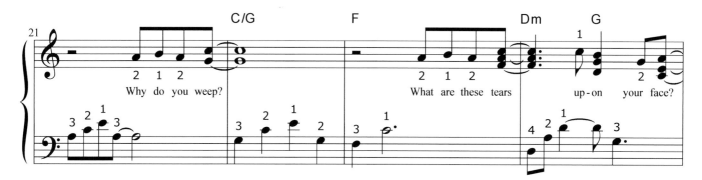

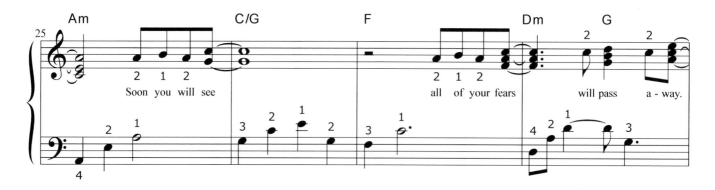

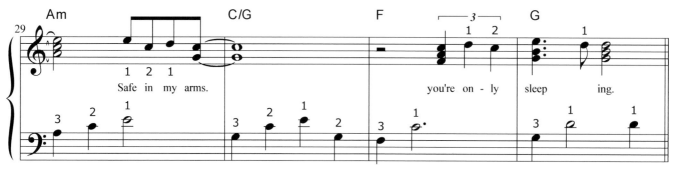

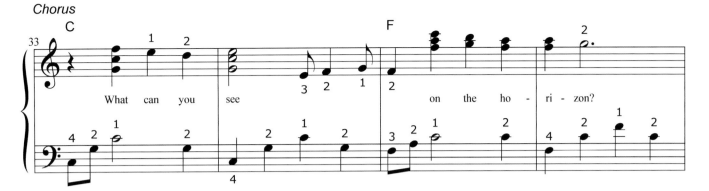

What can you see on the ho - ri - zon?

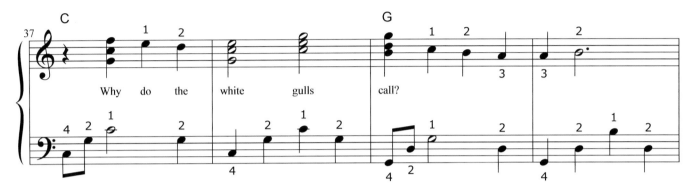

Why do the white gulls call?

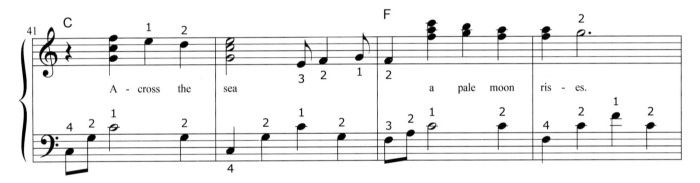

A - cross the sea a pale moon ris - es.

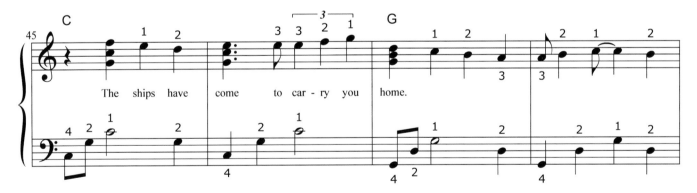

The ships have come to car - ry you home.

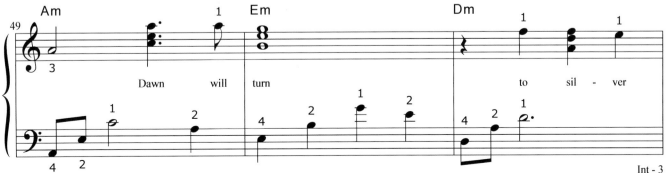

Dawn will turn to sil - ver

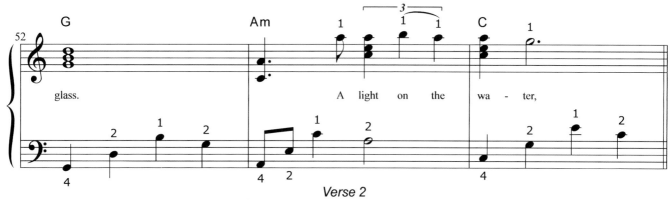

Verse 2

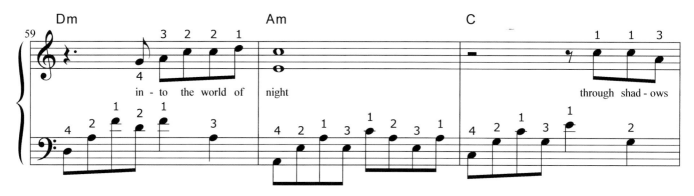

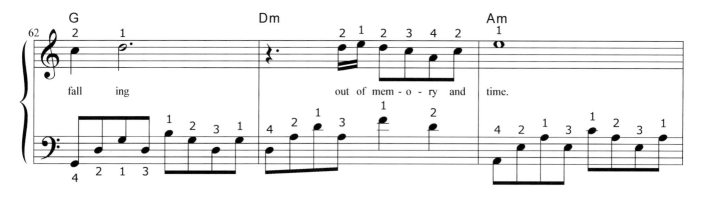

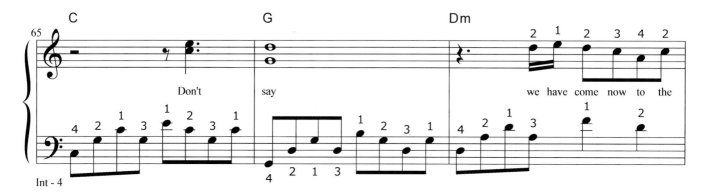

Int - 4

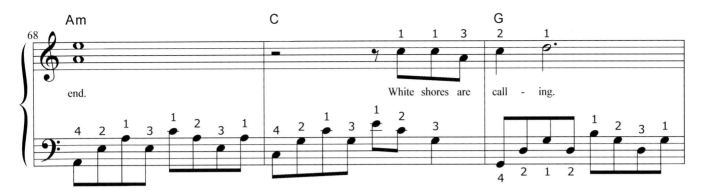

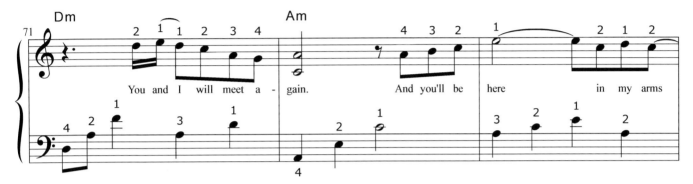

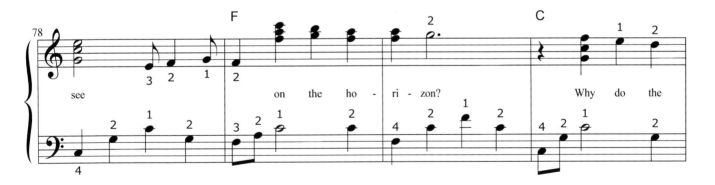

Int - 5

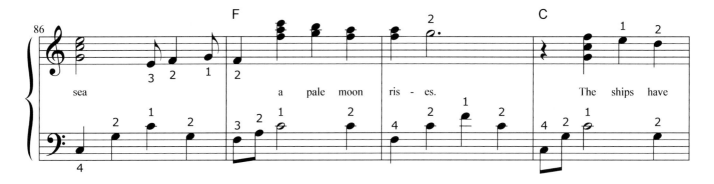

sea   a pale moon ris - es.   The ships have

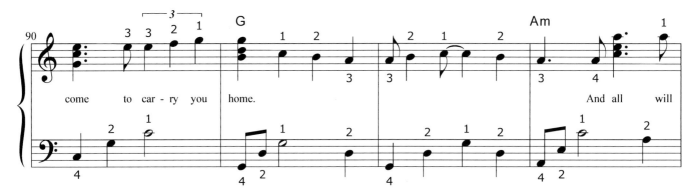

come to car - ry you home.   And all will

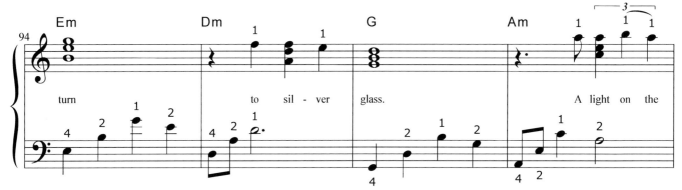

turn   to sil - ver glass.   A light on the

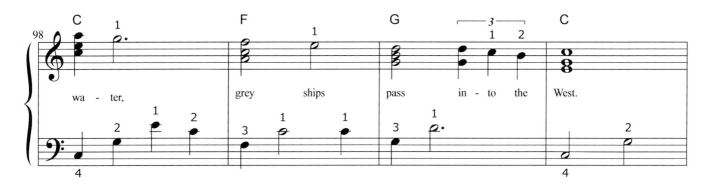

wa - ter,   grey ships   pass in - to the West.

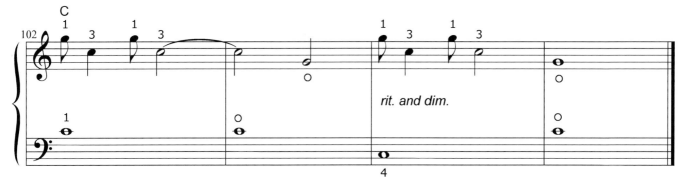

rit. and dim.

Int - 6